D1007144

THE RESPONSE OF WEEDS

"In these poems, Bickersteth invites the reader to revisit the prairies as landscape, but also as part of Black history, geography, and psychic and poetic space. Readers lucky enough to travel with him through these lands will discover new meanings and agricultures (in every sense of the word), as well as uncomfortable and exquisite truths as Bickersteth retells the prairies and makes them new again. This is an essential book by an enormously talented writer."

SUZETTE MAYR
author of *Dr. Edith Vane and the Hares of Crawley Hall*

"*The Response of Weeds* draws us into a confluence of geography, music, and identity, in which the voices of 20th Century Black artists fluidly merge with the prairies. In Bickersteth's interpretation we hear a blue modality and we feel Alberta sung as a point of arrival and departure, a junction in the diaspora. This collection questions place and belonging as it amplifies the Black prairie."

KAIE KELLOUGH
author of *Magnetic Equator*

"In *The Response of Weeds*, Bertrand Bickersteth is our wayfarer, drawing us—and the West Africans called 'Americans' he's tracking—across once-innocent prairies and lethal frozen landscapes in an exploration of our colonial, colonized Canadian history, and of ourselves. To whatever degree he's drawing upon his Sierra Leonean transatlantic perspective, he imparts a vision that is microscopic, telescopic, and kaleidoscopic, bearing witness to the pain and the beauty from the uncomfortably near and the philosophically far, and letting it all reflect back upon itself, and us. His verse, finely hewn, glitters with light that both dazzles and burns. He's the CanLit I never got to experience in all my time in school and university. If the CanLit gatekeepers will finally accept that literature doesn't need gated communities, Bertrand Bickersteth should be welcomed at every door."

MINISTER FAUST
Kindred Award-winning author of *Shrinking the Heroes*

THE
RESPONSE
OF WEEDS

A MISPLACEMENT OF BLACK POETRY ON THE PRAIRIES

BERTRAND BICKERSTETH

NeWest Press

Library and Archives Canada Cataloguing in Publication
Title: The response of weeds : poems / Bertrand Bickersteth.
Names: Bickersteth, Bertrand, 1969– author.
Description: Series statement: Crow said poetry series
Identifiers: Canadiana 20190167629 | ISBN 9781988732794 (softcover)
Classification: LCC PS8603.I326 R47 2020 | DDC C811/.6 – dc23

Board editor: Kit Dobson
Book design: Natalie Olsen, Kisscut Design
Cover photos: © Evil Pixels Photography and kkgas /Stocksy.com
Author photo: © Nathan Elson

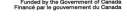

NeWest Press acknowledges the Canada Council for the Arts, the Alberta Foundation for the Arts, and the Edmonton Arts Council for support of our publishing program. This project is funded in part by the Government of Canada. ❡ NeWest Press acknowledges that the land on which we operate is Treaty 6 territory and a traditional meeting ground and home for many Indigenous Peoples, including Cree, Saulteaux, Niitsitapi (Blackfoot), Métis, and Nakota Sioux.

#201, 8540 – 109 Street Edmonton, Alberta T6G 1E6
780.432.9427
NEWEST PRESS www.newestpress.com

No bison were harmed in the making of this book.
Printed and bound in Canada   1 2 3 4 5   22 21 20

For anyone who has had to answer to
(various versions of) "where are you from?"

CONTENTS

Dramatis Historicae (Negro)

Dramatis Historicae (Negro)

LOUIS 'LOUIE' ARMSTRONG (1901–1971) revolutionary jazz trumpeter often considered a musical genius in the jazz world.

KATHLEEN BATTLE (1948–) pioneering opera singer, controversially accused of being contentious.

HENRY BIBB (1815–1854) prominent writer, journalist, publisher, and abolitionist who escaped to Canada, more than once.

STEPHEN (1799–1884), **GEORGE** (1802? –1874), and **PIERRE BUNGO** (circa 1770–1831), also **BONGA, BONZA, BOUGA**, black fur trading family; Stephen is one of the first recorded black people in Alberta.

MILES DAVIS (1926–1991) possibly the most famous jazz musician of all time.

RALPH ELLISON (1914–1994) esteemed writer from Oklahoma, one of Black Alberta's points of origin.

MATTHEW HENSON (1866–1955) explorer and author of *A Negro Explorer at the North Pole* (1912).

BILLIE HOLIDAY (1915–1959) influential jazz singer and gifted melodic interpreter.

LANGSTON HUGHES (1902–1967) one of the central figures of the Harlem Renaissance, and though established in New York, a prairie boy, born and raised.

DANIEL LEWIS (1888–1971) younger brother of Mildred Lewis, see below.

SYLVESTER LONG, aka **CHIEF BUFFALO CHILD LONG LANCE** (1890–1932) athlete, writer, actor, journalist, who asserted his Indigenous ancestry over his African American upbringing.

HATTIE MCDANIEL (1895–1952) actor for radio, television, and film, and the first African American to win an Oscar.

CLARENCE HORATIO MILLER, aka 'BIG' MILLER (1922–1992) Edmonton jazz singer, bassist, and trombonist originally from Kansas.

DAVE MILLS (1855–1918) the son of Henry Mills, Dave was raised among the Kainai of southern Alberta.

HARRY MILLS (1887–1962) the son of Dave Mills, and unofficial historian of his own family.

HENRY MILLS (1808–1878) fur then whiskey trader working on both sides of the Montana/Alberta border during the 1860s and 1870s.

JESSYE NORMAN (1945–) another pioneering opera singer, has been performing for nearly five decades.

PAUL ROBESON (1898–1976) legendary singer, actor, cultural and social(ist) icon.

JOHN WARE (1845?–1905) arguably Alberta's most famous cowboy (in fact, my paucity here is laughable).

MILDRED LEWIS WARE (1871–1905) Alberta pioneer, adapted to rural life, balancing the books, rearing five children, and occasionally acting as her husband's (John's) surrogate pen.

DANIEL WILLIAMS (1823–1887) a trader and trapper who lived in Peace country during the latter half of the 19th century.

RIVERS

*They talked to us about music and said it was the
only business that seemed proper for a Negro.*

— FROM —
*Big's Blues, unpublished autobiography
by Horatio 'Big' Miller*

FEATURING

John Ware

Daniel Williams

Daniel Lewis

Matthew Henson

Stephen Bungo

Jessye Norman

Kathleen Battle

Paul Robeson

The Negro Speaks of Alberta

Once, he stood on the banks of the Bow
near the confluence of the Oldman
watching for the common effluence of
the South Saskatchewan, the Red Deer,
the Saskatchewan, and so on
and on and on.

I know these rivers that flow past me
I've peered over their banks and know you do not see me

Once, he stood on the banks of this twisted river,
released a gleaming arc of relief into its heart.
For an untroubled while
their waters flowed together
and emptied together
out of a distant, unsuspecting mouth.

I know these rivers that flow through me
I've peered into their hearts and still you do not see me

What We Used to Call It

and that's not all, have you seen this one this place this prairie's face
look at its
                            wide   open   spaces

                its Chinook arched above
unclaimed coulees its snow covered skin

ice white riddled carapace dotted dirt yellow its singular snow owls
sentinels on
                                                      unexpected
                telephone
                poles

                            and that there is Nigger John's Creek but
we don't call it that anymore and this

                here is the end of the Bar U Trail and this and (and) this
here is the shadow of the Stoney

mountains cutting
                across unforgiving winter ground
                                            and this here is the
ground itself now   dead to the

drip of wheat sounding in its summer soul and the braids of oil coursing
through its

                golden veins and this vein yeah and (and and) that's not
all *that* there is where

I (I'm pretty sure) would be
                            long, if I only knew

                                    what that there is called.

I know what we used to call it.

The Peace

It is 1873, flowing along the Peace
from its source waters to Greater Slave Lake,
to the Mighty Mackenzie, to the patient body
of the Arctic. Along the way, at
Fort St. John, what do you see?

A raving negro, silently
signifying angry
but too far away for you to heed.
Something about claiming Native land
before the Hudson's Bay Company's claim.

It is perhaps the way of things
up here, up north
in Canada.
To tolerate his noise and then try
to drown it with your Peace.

But Negro Dan would know something
about a basinal baptism
with his bottomless Bible
and his ready quotes mussing up
your headwaters, signifying, angry.

Is it his fault that he reads
so much like a river Caliban
projecting his peaceful poxes
forcing you to take Notis? Have you
never wondered where these headwaters begin?

Legend has it that he married a Beaver
chief's daughter, who was struck
mute until that North-West Mounted Police
bullet struck her down
before it could strike her spirit husband, crying *stop*.

He is only too aware that this Peace
eventually becomes the Slave
an easing confluence
that confuses complaint in this country,
that always empties, quietly northward.

And here, finally, is Peace Point,
the zone we can never escape,
the collision of the Slave and the Peace.
A Canadian confounding that roils
unpronounced under Dan's proclamation.

Let me translate for him:
this is my Peace of country
if you know what's good
for you

watch your step!

Notice

featuring Blairmore Enterprise, April 24, 1919

NOTICE IS HEREBY GIVEN that I
Daniel Lewis, of Blairmore, in the Province
of Alberta, intend to apply for a
transfer of license from Michel Rosse to
myself, to operate a pool room on Lot 3
in Block 4, Plan 3319-I, on Victoria
Street, Blairmore. This application has
been approved by James G. Ewan,
mayor   DANIEL LEWIS,
                                          Applicant

So let me translate:

anything y'all do
I can do too

Watch my step!

The Athabasca

We might fall on this side of
the continental divide
but even our waters defy
the latitude of gravity
following no one flowing
on the uplift drift Northward
and not east or west
or south.

And did you know that it
comes to its near-death
in a northern delta, enclosed
from the coast
stranded on impertinent land
before it slips past and joins
the Slave on its implacable escape
to the North?

No Mississippi heat. No growling
Delta Bluesmen
unless you count that gathering
of into-it Inuit
over there and hear *her*
in the core of the *choeur*
reforging growl into *gorgeous*
by intuiting some inquisitive ancestors
maybe Thule and Matthew Henson
maybe, Negro of the North.

She's got no woman
She's got no job
She's got no truck

She's got no dog
She's got no history
That no one knows
And it's too cold
For the blues

If she had only followed the river
against its inclination
she would have made it south to
the lesser of the slave lakes
landing eventually at Athabasca
Landing and happening to
land in circa 1915 would have
been surrounded by the warmth
of people who bring the blues
with their blood lines.

Landed in Athabasca, honey
Got no time to fool
Said I'm stopped in Athabasca
Ain't the kind to fool
Well I was game in Oklahoma but
That place was much too cool

We, too, read advertisements for
160 acres and no mule

Grown in Alberta

In Michigan
they will point to a spot
on the palm of their right
hand

when you ask
where are you from?

For Michiganders
the hand is the simulacrum
for substitute belonging.

First came the hand
then the map
then the hand again.

The map's handsome substitute.

But first-first came the cold
and then the mitten:
the map's handsome substitute.

On the Canadian prairies
the cold is your constant contender
the cold is always first-first.

Once I dreamed of an empty grain elevator
sheathed in brittle ice.
I wanted to get inside

but each time I chipped
at its door, I felt an enervating
pang in the hollow of my abdomen.

I wanted to get outside
but each time I chipped at its door, I saw a glinting
mirrored surface magnifying my actions.

Everything went cold
my breath
undusted diamonds suspended before me.

A landscape was hinted in its spaces.

I would have placed my hand up against it,
the curl of my fingers
settling along the foothills,

but at times like these you can't help thinking about
those prototype fools in stories
baring the substitute cold to their tongues,

the very wording of my verisimilitude belonging.

And, Canada, you would not believe
how often a Michigander
never asked me

where are you from?

The Bow

I only know rivers

Waters elongated to the unrumpled recitatif
of endless land
The Bow knows
Has tongued and grooved the firmament, baby,
of this Last Best

The Bow knows
Stoney and Sarcee
The Bow knows Blood
The Buffalo spilled beyond its banks

The Bow knows Crowfoot
his Belly
his Old Man
softens his reservations
curses his Mary

The Bow knows
Bungo
trickles over his chipped away Chippewa,
black and bisected by befuddled namings
by bemused memory
by his own fickle fur trading
With us? With them? Negro? Ojibwe?
Exposed by history? Or submerged below?

No ocean.
No tide.
No salt.
No sea. Too flat. Too far to see.

I only knows rivers, baby,
but what I only knows disturbs in me

King Kong on the Prairies

We've stopped paying him any mind
with nothing of any consequence
to climb.

What's the point, really?
Maybe we should have let him live.

Shot through the heart
with an elephant gun

we brought with us
when we came here.

The mound of his carcass
is the tallest obstacle
between here and Saskatchewan.

Before we shot him
we had given him a cowboy hat

an original white Russian Shumiatcher
that Smithbilt later built.

It doesn't quite look like a fleck
of white pus

from a dimpled
blackhead. From this distance.

I remember the King on his island.
Back then I was just one
of the Savages hired
to reinforce the symbolism
of his unfettered nature
for your cameras.
I was good at my job.
It's funny to think that
we understood our limits too well
back then
and that now
his serenity adds a special
something to this unbroken landscape.

Past the Surface of Whiteness

Now I'm looking at a field
coping under a
layering of spring snow.
A moment ago it was actual spring.
A moment before that
it was permanent winter.
Now I am led to believe
in the dumb patience of fields.
Not unintelligent
nor quiescent
but unhurried, hewn and hued in quiet.
If whatever dreams beneath
poked a tendril
of colour
past this new surface
it would provide a new birth
starving in a world of white.
Or startling.

Another River

Another flood happened
this year
They've been happening
more and more

When the surface is as
flat as
ground zero

a simple trick
can whelm
the land

And
a simple trickle
finding its
groove

overwhelms

The Battle versus the Red Deer

There were no role models
for my sister the opera singer while she was growing up
Of course, there was always Jessye versus Kathleen
A tragic archetype split into
an overgenerous dichotomy of choice
But two is always (one) more
than enough when we're singing on their territory

Now, head off east toward Hanna instead of Wainwright
and at some point you will dip
into the valley of the badlands
and come out shamefully youthed
with the distant past roiling in the soul of your throat
This is the true contest
Where you dig down deep
beneath the surface
beneath the silt
behind Robeson and the rest
rolling it out from source to mouth
and here hearing it:

we, too, wade in this water!

Noticing

Notice how
invisible black is
when
you grow it in
storied soil
deep and dark
nurtured by an
anecdotal composition
rooted in
gleysolic hyperbolic
and stemming from
weightless whiteness

Once you go back
you will never go black

from

anabolic anaphora
proleptic proliferations
significant insignality
inverted visibility
notice unnoticed

to

noticing how visible
black is
when
you grow it in storied soil

My prairied soil

My soil has known inverse
ancient and dark

My soil grows deep and dark
like the inverse

ON THE PRAIRIES

I always dreaded to pass through a prairie ...
but there I was, in the open prairie, where I could
see no possible way by which I could escape.

— FROM —
Narrative of the Life and Adventures of Henry Bibb,
An American Slave, Written by Himself

FEATURING

Louis Armstrong

Big Miller

Miles Davis

Billie Holiday

Sylvester Long

Henry, Dave, and Harry Mills

Mildred Lewis Ware

Clark Kent on the Prairies

And how about that, eh? After all,
he grew up here too. Or somewhere
else like
here. Cornfields were his playgrounds.
The echoes of spaciousness were
bandied about by minute wildlife
in his evening experience. Sure,
he could see for miles
in any direction.
And weren't these things our
familiar too?
Remember kryptonite?
The chronic weakness:
a chunk of the past
recast as the recurring
question of home.

Now I'm Looking, Now I'm Unaware

Now I'm looking at a field in Michigan
puzzling at the singularity
of its groove and green.
I am struck,
unaware of the would-be echo stuck in me.
Unaware that I am comparing this field
to one in Alberta
burnished gold and flat.

Christopher Columbus on the Prairies

You always wonder what you will see
next when you are the first to arrive.
He must have been disappointed,
though, when confronted with all that gold
growing in the fields.
Wild roses
Wild canola
Goldenrod
Golden wheat
At this point of his journeying
having achieved the very heartland of the continent
even the Great Discoverer
would have been getting tired of El Dorado myths.
It probably didn't occur to him that
walking the long walk back
to the boats would give him the opportunity
to misname the largesse
of his own luck.

Louis Armstrong on the Prairies

I'm telling you, man
the cat
skipped the prairies and went
straight to the mountain
and it never got too cold
for that
cat just spread some hot fives
and sevens
wherever there was a little ice.

Wailing, moaning, trumpeting
the cool front man blasted back
what
ever
cold front faced him
split
the air with his ambivalent grin
and warmth settled over this side
of *les Rocheuses*
like a blue note bath.

And what do you suppose he saw
dissolving with the warming of the snow?

The older impressions of Matthew Henson
a historical haint, headed further north.

And, no, it don't mean a thing, Louis,
if he ain't gotta swing through Banff.

North Pole Negro,
been here long ago?

Ain't it a wonderful world.

Now, *go*, Louis, and *tell* it!

Alberta Presents Big Miller

I never saw Big Miller play
Here is his impression though
One more silent invader who followed
the well worn-away ancient cattle trail
north
leaving invisible prints, following invisible prints
one more historical haint
soothing the South with nothing
but his bare hands and his giant Albertan presence

"So What?"

Harlem farming
So what
if these planed lands have no history?
We have no history
that we have not stolen
swallowed
misplaced
portaged

We're still portraying over here
Our pasts have always been
on the move
so Langston's groove
and Billie's blues

and John Ware's dues
have all been here before

Harlem farming
We read and reseed in spring
We flower in this generation
of winter with

the North on top
Everything is upside down, fellah
Harlem farming in Alberta
(upside down)

Miles and Miles from the middle of anywhere
I still mean business on this ground
This season, you should learn to reread my irritation
I still *mean* here

"So, where are you from?"

So
what

Sylvester Long on the Prairies

Never wanted to come here
but choice can force your hand,
signals heteroglossia.
So, in the South
your story is known before you
are born.
So it is told while you
simmer silently.
And, so, it never ends.

The first section
is called how your ancestors
screwed up
(and down
the steps
of respectability).
The next section
is for coloreds only
also known as the balcony

and even though you were
politely pointed upward,
you remanipulated
the gesture, stepped
outside, made straight
for open grass
and kept right on running,
fleeing farther and faster even
than your own Blackfeet could carry you.

Three Mills on the Prairies:
Henry Mills, Specialized in Trades

No nonsense knowing – he knew the score.
Slavery: ten – Emancipation: zero.

Ended up almost ownerless in Montana
and, quite naturally, became a trapper.

He began with furs. Snatching work and worth
from the American Fur Company.
Then, he cornered a wife right on the Blood
reserve. Then another. But his first, most
sacred apprehension, surely, was when
he caught that invasive whiff of freedom.
So strange, so foreign, at first, a crisis
soon refashioned to opportunity.

You gotta keep elevating yourself
up the longitudinal trail. You won't fail
to get noticed. "Ran Away. Henry Mills
on the 10th, ultimo, from his Master,
he fled precipitately from his work
in the fear of a deserved correction.
Very tall. Very dark black complexion.
Answers to Harry. Ten dollars reward."

He mastered traps but he specialized in
trades:
Canada for the us.
White master for red mistress.
Whipped hide for tanned fur.
Hudson's Bay Company
for American Fur Company.
One Blood wife here
for another back
there in the us
again.
Jibbered English
for jabbered

Kainai.
Bidding
for biding.
Work
for time.
Word
for rhyme.

Stay
alive
past
'65

then take your children and your freed ass to the edge
of the reserve and leave them there.

Three Mills on the Prairies:
Dave Mills, on the Edge of the Reserve

featuring Harry Mills

i.

My father was a good interpreter.
He used plain simple language and wasn't
afraid to admit when he was wrong.

When an Indian came into the Agency

he would give his name in Black
feet, my father would translate it, and the
clerk would write it down. One day an Indian

came in and gave his name. It was "Pooks-see-see."

Without thinking, my father gave it the
correct translation. "Small Asshole," he told
the clerk. "What?" said the clerk, jumping up from

his desk. So my father repeated it.

"I can't write that down," he said. "We would spoil
the books with a name like that." Anyway,
the clerk decided to put it down as

Small Backside.
But later
they changed it

again to Not Good.

ii.

Scabby Bull
stood between two people
The Pikanu and the Sioux

and the white people.
Which one are you?
they cried to the Blackman.
Which one are you?

Pikanu.
He lied.

And every
one sighed.

Nobody died
that day.

Maybe he suspected his
Blackman's blood
line from day to

day was beginning its wane.

Nor was he a black-whiteman
like his father
but managed to lie

just where old Henry had left him

on the edge of the reserve
for the rest of his life

where, luckily,
we eventually

uncovered him.
So, nobody's

Blood blackline
dies to

day.

Good.

Three Mills on the Prairies:
Harry Mills, the Music is Passing

Said he's a real old timer
with one mean old scowl
Yes he's a real old timer
with one mean old scowl
Can holler his hey-yah
but ain't got no howl

'Cause the blues is all gone
from under his skin
Said the blues is all gone
from under his skin
The music is passing
gone dark, like his kin

Brother up and died
just when his daddy did
Said his brother done passed
when his daddy did
In the 191st battalion
like any darkie kid

And his mammy's unknown
to any known text
Said his mammy's not known
in any kinda text
No name for the last
No name for the next

You can knock 'em straight
but he'll throw you a curve
Said, if you whack 'em straight
Harry lets loose a curve
Done cakewalked his Blood-line
from the edge to the reserve

Milk River

Don't look right.
It don't look white
to me. Look
at that
colour
            of water.
The slip
streaming of
untouchable colour.
Undrinkable ilk.
Around St. Mary's,
across the dam
and maybe, eventually, into
Ol' Miss
Herself.
These old white
ladies turned toward
the opposite
but still touching finger
tips.
Ol' Miss
And Princess Louise.
Tipping points of history
erasing our
reflections.

A few girls sit near a copse
beside a jetty
with their dragging playful circles
spinning stories
on the surface.

The water rushes on
from America
and back to America
in between
graced by the meting out
of mere child's play.

There is a story that says
the waters from all of the rivers
of North America
have their source in the centre of the
prairies.

A vast plain of natural nurturing
the udder of otherness
hidden in plain sight
black gigantic
water mother
creation creature.

And that rivers are the entrails
of its otherness
freed of colour

Still don't look white
to me
thinks one of the girls dragging
the line of a leaf through expanding
concentric momentum
watering southward
eventually emptying
this Canadian creation
into that Milkified Mississippi
Delta.

The Last Step

John Ware
out on the range with his boy
and his horse
stepped in it

That hollowed presence
in the prairie floor
killed him
Mildred died six months before

My people, watch your step!

NOW I'M THE ONE THAT'S LOOKING

*Atoh had a roving, studied look that gave many
a vain person the impression of being scrutinized.*

— FROM —
"Night, Joe" by Esi Edugyan

FEATURING

Henry Bibb

These Empty Flatlands

Now I'm looking
at a field.
There is a scarecrow looking
back at me.
We look at each other.
Two straw men
marking out the edges of these empty flatlands
stuffed with their essence.
Then I notice
the scarecrow
has no face
has no eyes
is not interested in looking
is not capable
of seeing me.

The Wrongness of a Word

Now I'm looking at fields outside of Olds
on the 2A somewhere
after Didsbury or before Carstairs
somewhere. Summer's height.
Those swaying green giants will be cut for hay
and the aroma of their release
will speak the certainty of its place.
My eyes do not resist
the gentle settling darkness
bespeak the settling darkness
pinks and oranges deepening in the sky
deeper still.
My place is with the oncoming
darkness of the night.
It is funny how a word
even the wrongness of a word
can speak things
into a simple and instant order.
Like the nig that wrongly
speaks of night. It's quiet deepening.
Still. Here I am again
labouring words over a vast simplicity
I refuse to name as beauty.
Night settles over these rippling fields.
Beauty is black.

The Magpie's Place

Even these quiet moments are visited
by questions of faith
and the integrity of justice

Why should anyone believe in a natural
eventfulness of simple good
in the simplicity of everyone?

For here and here are occurrences
of egregious failings,
and despite our systems

our democratic aspirations, inventing,
our weighted anticipations, enshrined
in policy, trial, and treaty

we fail repeatedly

in the cherishing of this human
and that one, here and here,
whether the cherishing is anticipated

through our institutions
or performed in misunderstood
sacred rituals, daily tasks,

such as providing encouragement
to those we see as better than ourselves
in every way

or doing the dishes because we recognize
that we normally don't do the dishes,
normally don't give their doing a thought

Bad faith — Is this bad faith?

I think a man hurled out a word
a few weeks ago that named me
Despite everything, it remains undismissed

undismissible in my mind
By "despite everything" I mean
our weighted anticipations

as well as our misunderstood sacred rituals
as I've already mentioned
So, the victim of singular syllables?

Or the progenitor of a bad faith?
Where is the quiet inside the storm
inside these quiet moments

set off, this time, by a simple magpie
playing before me, completely
unfettered to her blackness and whiteness?

A thing of natural cherishing
Listen to her ugly caw
divorced from its ugliness

Look at her undismissible place
sometimes the spirit of playfulness
sometimes the bullet of purpose

shot across the sky
drawing my eye inward
to some darkness

some question I try to anticipate
in the sensual heaviness
of summer aroma

the rippling gold of canola
the single stalk, right, in its place
the cherishing across each field

The North Saskatchewan

Ferry across
fifteen cents one
way a quarter
return

but can't go at the same time as him
can I?

It's fine. Negroes
are human too.

But not exactly human. Obviously, they're not the same
as us.

No, they are not the same as the white man
who has conquered all others and is the master of
sciences, technologies, arts, history, and civilization.

True, they are not quite the same as us.

I don't think they can come on with us. I don't think
it's allowed.

It is allowed.

Well I don't think
it should be.

Me neither. They're dangerous. It's in their blood. They can't help it.
You see it in the papers
all the time. I mean,
I got nothing against them personally
and back on the farm
I used to live down the road from a family of negroes
and the mammee, Auntie something or other we called her, she
would do our laundry on the weekends,
and my younger brother used to go to school with her young'uns
so I know what I'm talking about. I know these people. Sure some of them
are nice but sooner or later something's gonna rise in the blood. They
can't help it. It can't
be helped if they're not civilized. Like us.

Yeah, I remember the newspaper articles about that girl
who was taken and oh lord I can't even speak of it the horror
it brings to mind. But you all remember. She was taken by
that wild negro and there was a manhunt
and everything.

I remember that. It was a hoax. Remember? The girl had lost her
mother's ring.

That's right, he stole a ring! Broke into her house and stole —

It was a hoax. The girl was covering up. Lost it herself.
So she said a negro broke in and stole it.
Remember?

Oh. Yeah. I remember. So I'm not talking about *that* time but you know
all the others that you hear about or read about
in the news.

I still maintain, ladies and gentlemen,
although the negro is an inferior human being, certainly inferior
to the white man,
he is still a human being.
In which case, he is free to join us on this ferry
so long as he pays the asked for fee.

Look, he's got money!

Probably stole it.

I can't wait until they finish building that high
bridge over there. Then we won't be forced to share company
with any common ruffian
on this ferry.

Yes, if he slits our throats in the middle of the river we'll have
you to thank, Doctor.

Madame, he wouldn't dare. We are within a stone's
throw view of Mr. Walter's house
at the bottom of the hill. Do you not see it?

Besides, these are not the lawless United States of America. The negro
will not slit throats out of fear
for our law and order. You need not expect an influencing factor
from Dixieland. We are Canadians! Therefore, Mr. Wooly Head
is free to cross on the ferry with us.

With the fee!

With the fee.

So long as it wasn't stolen!

It wasn't stolen Mr. Wooly Head, was it?

     No, suh.

There you have it, Madame. Polite as a pickaninny.
You shall have no
problems though
the river is wide.

I guess.

And

been guessing

ever

since.

The Lingering Look

Now I'm looking at a field of wheat
that was.
Only the husked stumps and
a straw-like scattering of crisp gold
remain.
Somehow, it is the lingering look of violence.
A pillaging, a ripping has taken place.
Somehow, a ripple of glee thrills through me
at the sight of this reasonable violence
and its leftover roots
waiting for the next opportunity.

Henry Bibb on the Prairies

The price of a really good run

Stick to the bush
Find a wood
marsh
or swamp

Get stuck in
Keep running

When your shack of ribs
is fit to burst and each breath
a knife through your throat
keep running

Ignore the spectral rattles of death
mimicking your moves
haunting the bruised footfalls
each battered beat between your feet
a chorus for the lusting paddy rollers
their feline dogs
their lust

Keep running
Know the North Star by heart

Don't look up
Don't dream into the night sky
or question the contrast of
sparkling glories against
inky firmament
or aspire

One day you *may* be free
but you will never outrun the skein of the skin
your contrast will always be revealed,
your freedom, reveiled, so

at all costs understand your opportunities

Avoid the open prairie

The Oldman

Rifts right
through
the heart
of some Piikani

pickaninny
song Wraps

his
hearing
around
Kainai cliffs Weaves

melodies Works
songs Slaves
over exchanged
ancestors Shares
our
surety Knows

Bow
and Belly
and Belly
knows Bow

This Oldman has
a belly
has no belly
has a stone has
no stone has
writing
has
no writing-on

is only
voice to *sing*
Napi
sing

Second Sightings

Now I'm looking at a field as flat
and far-flung as Saskatchewan
over there.
This is my first sighting of this
particular field.
I know it yet.
Without reflection or remembering
or effort of any sort
the image of this field relaxes
against some familiar notch in my brain.
Maybe it is because this is my
particular hole
in the wall
the space where I belong.
Maybe it is because I *have* seen it
missing
in that classic movie
with Nipsey and Michael
and Diana and
the fickle snowstorm that displaces each of us.

Don't Forget These Things

Now I'm waiting on a park
bench for a friend of mine to come
and also, for all that,
for the stiffening cold
in a late summer breeze
and for the indifferent hardening of earth
and for the fear for finding food
that animals feel
and for the crinkled feel
of rejection that all things solid take on
over the course of a season
used to over-exposure
and for the brittle air,
emptied of warmth.
Eh? Don't forget these
things belong here too.

Harlem Farming

North of the Lower East Side
is the Upper West Side.
North of the Upper West Side

Harlem
the historical heart
the A Train
the Renaissance
the Great Day
the Apollo Theater
the UNIA Parades
the Boys Choir
the Dance Theatre
Martin Luther King Jr. Boulevard
the Great Migration

North of Harlem
farming
in Saskatchewan and Alberta

Obviously

Space Overhungry for City

Now I'm looking at a row of would-be empty lots
all fulfillments of city plans
all filled with cornrow upon cornrow
of suburban dwellings
before they had a chance to
be empty
before they had a chance
to collect in garish piles
the sheen of industry
and the persistence of proliferation
cast in the same lot:

pvc piping
layers of lumber
milk weeds
whose sproutings only need a few days
to look like they have always belonged
like they were
                        here
first.

And these rookie rows of cookie
cutter houses on the edges of our
unhindered cities
seem to say something familiar:
these empty lots are a
restless anticipation
of space overhungry for city
that gorges on city
that projects city
that moves not with the energy
of a sprawling
but the action of emptiness
scattering at the speed
of seed.

ACCIDENTAL AGRICULTURE

Sometimes I wish I lived in the States ...
At least I wouldn't have to walk around
in a sea of White faces there.

— FROM —

Pourin' Down Rain by Cheryl Foggo

FEATURING

Ralph Ellison

Hattie McDaniel

Language Like Holes

Damned Pi
that bastard
spawned in likeliness
swathed in blackness
yet, between
$3\frac{1}{7}$ and $3\frac{10}{71}$,

is *somewhere*
in there
sometimes sitting
still
outpacing
your gazing
belonging beyond
wholes
and captive only
to language-like
holes.

Out of Darkness

Honey, today I came
out of darkness
with black ahead
black behind
Said I came
out of darkness
black in front
black behind
but I'm sitting
here now that's what
you'll find
strange words
ahead
strangeness
behind
that's what
you'll find

stranger words
black behind

Alberta, my woman, says
where you been

all night
waiting, waiting
all night

She says
calling, calling
where did you go?

I was looking for you

And stranger than strange
the funny thing is,
I've just been sitting here holding her hand
It feels alive
It feels cold
It's a feeling I don't understand

Just sitting, here, more alone than alone
holding court
from the absent throne
scratching scrap-like silences
to quiet the darkness

But I come from darkness
the darkness surrounds
My heart is darkness
darkness is my sound
I make sense in the darkness
Walls collapse in darkness
And like a somnambulist
I stand up unscathed
Unscathed by the darkness
but not unchanged
by the wronging of the light
(I will write it again)
by the wronging of the light

Alberta, my woman, says
Where you been

all night
waiting, waiting
all night

She says
calling, calling
where did you go?

I was looking for you

But, I said, surprised
I'm always looking for *you*
But she couldn't hear

You disappeared! She was scared

My head was adjusted
My hair was a mess
My words came off backwards
My clothes were distressed

Confess, my love nightmare
just confess
Put down that paper
put down your pen
tell it all from the start

Again, I say, I was looking for *you*
I don't know what happened next

I was holding your hand, then
I fell into something beautiful
that I couldn't see
I became something unfathomable
that you couldn't read

And before my woman could say
another word
I held up my hand

But she just couldn't see
the pen, the paper, the every
thing that was me

Honey, I have been in darkness
I have lived with fear
but I was born from darkness
and now I am
here

Seeing Only Absence

Now I'm looking at a field flashing
by that looks like wheat.
We both look at its familiar shape
seeing only absence
instead of fuzzy tops, instead
of accidental afro-*cum-Triticum*.
We stare into the extra pinkish tones
the orange angles added
seeing only the addition.
Wordless, we return our eyes to the
inevitable highway
the single line that is everywhere always
hoping onward on these flatlands.
The undivided line between
whatever weirdness worrying one's landscape
and
whatever.

Teen Preaching

Don't cross me whitey
Don't see me
Black cow poke
Prairie posture

Me, the undivided line

The gaze across the empty railroad tracks
says it all

Black head banged
Prairie rocked

Dreaded but locked
out in the open

Hanged by language
(this lynching is a cinch
sings a two-step in
the undivided line dance)

Gangless and harangued
Teenage tribe of one
and maybe one
("oh, is that your brother?")

Out here, where one and one
makes none
more brooding
none more *sensitive*
(more cross)
than a gang of none
at a loss for hoards

Black oil baron
Prairie prayin'

"So sorry! Didn't see you all
there," they say and replay

in their banter
their joking storm
in their scripts
in their songs

The normal folks
who stride across the badlands of the norm,
looking back, wonder where exactly they
stepped in it

The brooding anger of none,
breeding, always leaves some
thing behind

"Jeez, I said *sorry* — Jeez, eh!"

And so we multiply the indivisible:
until we cross the line
it stays invisible

The Invisible Man on the Prairies

featuring Ralph Ellison

No one sees this, no
but he is a part of this
landscape too.
Right here. Here, right
in front of your long nose.
Not impressed?
It's no trick.
Hold out your hand and
move it back
and forth
in history.
He is still going to be there
and here.
What a sight not to behold!
His OK
your AB
See?

Anything and everything
was to be found in the chaos
of Oklahoma; thus

the concept of the Renaissance
Man has lurked long within

the shadow of my past

See?
The shadow in the act
that is what you
feel haunting your hand
(you can pull it back now).
Impressed?
(You will be.)

More than just looked over
he is inverted presence
that unexpectedly
shapes
the landscape you
walk on

unrevealed
unvisible
unwholed.

Watch your step!

The Typical Spirit

featuring Emily Murphy

A short while ago
a negro

in a Western Canadian city, with the typical expansive spirit of the
prairies, purchased

350 suitcases
in one day.

Seed Catalogue

Canola mustard wheat
hay the seed catalogue
written by Kroetsch

Maybe

I can plant something with *that*

Because its Season is Short

Growing up in the city
I never looked at nature.
Now, when I look at fields,
I see.
Our eyes are fuller with the failure
of the past brimming in our sight.
Ignorance, lassitude, indifference
now all look
iridescent, variegated,
teeming
like the bloom
on that Heuchera Obsidian
Coral Bell swollen with colour
because its season
is short
and it knows
it will never
be a bloom again.

Hattie McDaniel on the Prairies

Here is a message from you
to Oscar.
Tell him
you understand masks better than he does
because there is nowhere to hide
when you are out on the prairies.
And you were a Kansan, born on the prairies.

Tell him that if he notices you
shining his shoeless stump
with your name placarded to its pedestal
not to confuse your joy with the roles
scripted out for you. Ok, there's nothing
new here, Oscar, but your *notis* is the first
of its kind and, frankly,
Mammy don't give a damn
that we ain't in Kansas no more.
Just like the script says.

The Blindman

This man
slyly
sidles

eyes silent

formates
pas-ka-poo

mouths
red deer

wanders

currently
english
knowingly
cree
site
un
sightly

swirls
swerves
southward
homing in
meanders
meward and

swears

like every gushing
revisionary
"I don't see

colour,"
man

Accidental Agriculture

The bruising beginning
face rubbed in
Alberta's finest
Orthic Dark Brown Chernozem
where wheat flourishes
and barley wails

After the fight
we congregate in the principal's office:
punishments
meted out to him
the aggressor
who impugned my face against the ground
because its darkness inspired
a simile
part-time prairie poet he was

And punishments
meted out to me
the victim so called

Well, why did you fight back?
Why do you people
always fight?
Now I have to punish you
too

The principal glares at me
his eyes a shock
of literal blue

Outside
on my way home
I pondered the view
from the top of a rare hill
an indifferent field spilled
with dandelions was splayed out below

This accidental agriculture
will be swallowed
by an instantaneous city
its inevitability
its ignorance

I saw the whole against the horizon

a nine-year-old
a timeless landscape
a flatness ensuing

My tender head still throbbing
from the blunt encounter
I reached with a quiet fist
to rub at the soreness swelling
around my eyes

Well
why *did* you fight back?

When the black child is six years old
in Harlem
he suddenly sees everything he has been before
and all that was sown before him and

how

it has been sown before him and
this
my muse
James Baldwin
muses
is the fundamental difference between

any child growing anywhere
in Alberta

and the child that must see things
through black eyes

Noticed

Dan worned Kenedy
he shal Not betrubbled
Nor trod on
except by her most Noble
                    Majesty

Because Kenedy toer-Down
that Notis

and now it is
Dan's turn to tore down

so watch his step

And Daniel advised
the public
getting up and in
his business
that they

can watch his step

But I should have translated
the anticipation in anger

and not just the whir
of their words

What I meant to impress:

Y'all may be
here

but *we*
                    all
still be
long

A Note on Names

When I was thirteen, my best friend at the time, a wiry, energetic, entrepreneurial and truly imaginative youth, tried to convince me that I was not a "nigger." This naming, he explained, was for pimps or drug dealers or certain kinds of crooks. "You are not a nigger," he continued. "You're my friend. My best friend. I can use the worst word for you and you can use the worst word for me. It doesn't matter. We're just friends."

I had no answer for that, but I did spend much mental energy trying to conceive of the 'worst word' I could apply to him if we were to go down that road. Cracker? Whitey? Honky? I was powerless to know.

This was one of my many lessons in naming: words can enforce silence because namers have power. Some of these lessons have eventually led to the creation of *The Response of Weeds,* which is a grappling with history, race, place, and words themselves. And though much has been learned since I was a teenager, as you can see, neither I nor you have escaped sticks and stones in this collection of poems. Namings like "Negro," "Sarcee," "Savages," and, yes, worse grace these pages.

Words, certainly, can be bad when they under or overexplain, categorically. Words can be even worse when they do both at the same time. But the worst words? They can be capable of poetry. As a thirteen-year-old, black Albertan, it was impossible for me to imagine the worst words for the white, teenage boy who named me "not-nigger." But I can now:

Best friend.

Acknowledgments

Several of the poems rely on or quote from previously published materials. I would like to acknowledge the following poems and their sources:

"Notice" quotes from a public announcement in the *Blairmore Enterprise*, April 24, 1919 from Daniel Lewis, a relative of John Ware.

"Noticed" partially quotes from Butler's relating Dan Williams's notice to George Kennedy, the Hudson's Bay Company factor at Fort St. John. It is one of the earliest known recordings of authorship by a black Albertan. The quote is taken from page 218 of *The Wild North Land: Being the Story of a Winter Journey, with Dogs, Across Northern North America* written by Sir William Francis Butler and published in 1873.

"Three Mills on the Prairies: Henry Mills, Specialized in Trades" reworks a runaway slave notice from 1794. The original is available through the Hudson River Valley Heritage digital collection at the following address: www.hrvh.org/cdm/ref/collection/hhs/id/587.

"Three Mills on the Prairies: Dave Mills, on the Edge of the Reserve" quotes from a transcription of a 1963 interview with Harry Mills held by Alberta's eminent historian, Hugh Dempsey. I would like to express my sincerest gratitude to Mr. Dempsey for very generously providing me with a copy of his transcription.

"The Invisible Man on the Prairies" quotes from "Introduction" from SHADOW AND ACT by Ralph Ellison, copyright © 1953, 1964 and renewed 1981, 1992 by Ralph Ellison. Used by permission of Random House, an imprint and division of Penguin Random House LLC. All rights reserved.

"The Typical Spirit" quotes from page 150 of the 1922 Thomas Allen edition of *The Black Candle* by Emily Murphy.

The epigraphs for each section appear with the permissions from sources I would like to gratefully acknowledge here:

The epigraph featuring Big Miller appears courtesy of the Provincial Archives of Alberta, Big Miller fonds, PP2285, accession number PR2007.0437/0082.

Selection from "Night, Joe" is used by permission of Esi Edugyan.

Epigraph on p. 63 is from *Pourin' Down Rain* by Cheryl Foggo, Edmonton: Brush Education, 2020, p X. Copyright © Cheryl D. Foggo, 1990 and 2020. Used by permission of the publisher.

Many people have read versions of and commented on various poems in this collection. Among them I would like to acknowledge my editor, Kit Dobson, for his insights and judicious choices; Claire Kelly, the marketing and production coordinator at NeWest Press, for her perceptive proofing; Anne Burke for her meaningful encouragement and support; and my colleagues, Nikki Cook, Katie King, Keith Friedlander, and Brendan Richardson, for their willingness, interest, and enthusiasm.

Lastly, I would like to thank my parents, Patrick and Farrella, who seeded me as a writer; Paris, who is my s/weed; and Steen, who mysteriously does not see the need for poetry, but, maybe more mysteriously, does see the need for me.

In 2017, to honour NeWest Press' 40th anniversary, we inaugurated a new poetry series to go alongside our Nunatak First Fiction, Prairie Play, and Writer as Critic series: Crow Said Poetry. Crow Said is named in honour of Robert Kroetsch's foundational 1977 novel *What The Crow Said*. The series aims to shed light on places and people outside of the literary mainstream. It is our intention that the poets featured in this series will continue Robert Kroetsch's literary tradition of innovation, interrogation, and generosity of spirit.

CROW SAID POETRY TITLES AVAILABLE FROM NEWEST

Tar Swan — David Martin

That Light Feeling Under Your Feet — Kayla Geitzler

Paper Caskets — Emilia Danielewska

let us not think of them as barbarians — Peter Midgley

Lullabies in the Real World — Meredith Quartermain

The Response of Weeds: A Misplacement of Black Poetry on the Prairies — Bertrand Bickersteth

Born in Sierra Leone, Bertrand Bickersteth grew up in Edmonton, Calgary, and Olds, Alberta. After an English degree at UBC, Bertrand continued studying in the U.K. and later taught in the U.S. A return to Alberta provided him with new insights on black identity and most of his writing has been committed to these perspectives ever since. Although he writes in several genres, anticlimactically, the topic is always the same: what does it mean to be black and from the prairies? He has also given many public talks including a TED Talk for BowValleyCollegeTEDx called *The Weight of Words*. His poetry has appeared in several publications, including most recently *The Antigonish Review*, *Cosmonauts Avenue*, and *The Fieldstone Review*. He has also been published in *The Great Black North* and the forthcoming anthology *The Black Prairie Archives* (2020). In 2018, he was long-listed for the CBC Poetry Prize. He lives in Calgary, teaches at Olds College, and writes everywhere.